DAILY LIFE in Ancient Greece

by Lisa M. Bolt Simons

raintree
a Capstone company — publishers for children

Raintree is an imprint of Capstone Global Library Limited, a company incorporated in England and Wales having its registered office at 264 Banbury Road, Oxford, OX2 7DY – Registered company number: 6695582

www.raintree.co.uk
myorders@raintree.co.uk

Edited by Aaron Sautter
Designed by Bobbie Nuytten
Picture research by Svetlana Zhurkin
Production by Jennifer Walker

ISBN 978 1 4747 1744 1
19 18 17 16 15
10 9 8 7 6 5 4 3 2 1

British Library Cataloguing in Publication Data
A full catalogue record for this book is available from the British Library.

Photo Credits
Alamy: Mary Evans Picture Library, 13, North Wind Picture Archives, 9, 11, 19, 21; National Geographic Creative: H.M. Herget, cover (top), 7, 15; Newscom: Universal Images Group/Leemage, 14; Shutterstock: Arkady Chubykin, cover (bottom), 1, Dhoxax, 8, Emi Cristea, 18, Ensuper (paper), back cover and throughout, ilolab (grunge background), cover, 1, James Steidl, 20, Kamira, back cover (bottom right), Madlen, 12, Maxim Kostenko (background), 2 and throughout, mexrix, 5 (back), Roberto Castillo (column), back cover and throughout; Wikipedia: MatthiasKabel/Sting, 17; XNR Productions, 5 (map)

We would like to thank Jonathan M. Hall, professor at the University of Chicago, for his invaluable help in the preparation of this book.

Printed and bound in China.

Contents

GROWING UP IN ANCIENT GREECE

Imagine growing up in Greece 3,000 years ago. You wake up on a mattress filled with grass or feathers. If you're a boy, you may go to school. If you're a girl, a **tutor** teaches you at home instead. During free time you can play with your toys. These include clay figures, wax dolls or balls made from pig bladders. Welcome to life in ancient Greece!

FACT:

Students often did schoolwork on a wooden tablet that was filled with wax. They wrote on the wax with a bone or metal **stylus**. The wax could be smoothed out to erase the work and continue writing.

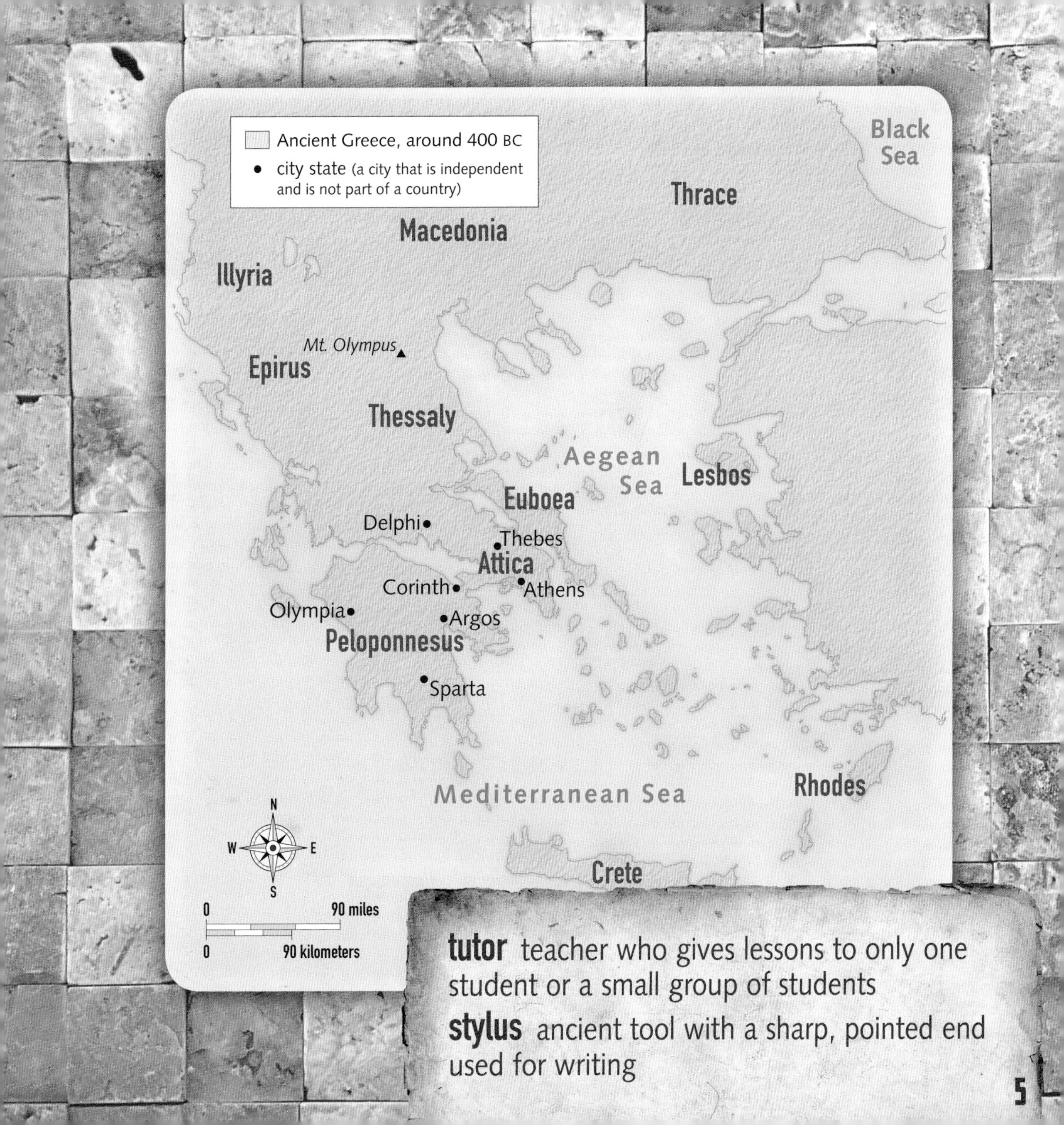

tutor teacher who gives lessons to only one student or a small group of students

stylus ancient tool with a sharp, pointed end used for writing

Whether rich or poor, people's lives were busy in ancient Greece. Children in **wealthy** families were usually sent to school or taught at home. But poor families usually made children do chores at home instead. Men fought in the army or had jobs outside the home. Most women stayed at home to run their houses or manage the family's **slaves**.

A FATHER'S DECISION

Greek fathers could choose to accept or reject a newborn baby. If he named the baby within 10 days of its birth, it became part of the family. But if he rejected the baby, it was often placed in a clay pot and left by the road. A different family could then adopt the baby.

boys attending school in Athens

wealthy having a great deal of money
slave person who is owned by another person and is forced to work without pay

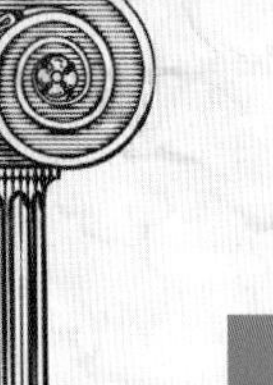

LIFE AT HOME

Clothing

Most families in ancient Greece made their own clothes. Everyone wore free-flowing clothes called **tunics**. Cloaks were also worn in cold weather. At first, nearly everybody's clothes were white. But people began to wear brightly coloured clothing around 500 BC. Some people wore strapped sandals or boots to protect their feet, but many went barefoot.

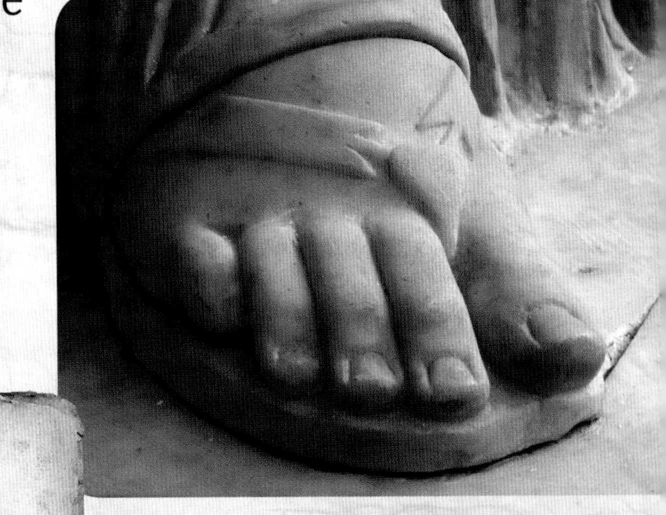

tunic loose, sleeveless garment

The ancient Greeks often wore colourful, loose-fitting clothing.

Houses

Ancient Greek houses were made of wood, mud bricks or stone. Two or three rooms were built around a **courtyard**. Men, women and children had separate rooms. Every house had an altar for making animal **sacrifices** to the gods. Most houses didn't have a bathroom. Instead, people used **chamber pots** or went outside.

courtyard open area surrounded by walls
sacrifice offering made to a god
chamber pot type of bowl that people used as a toilet

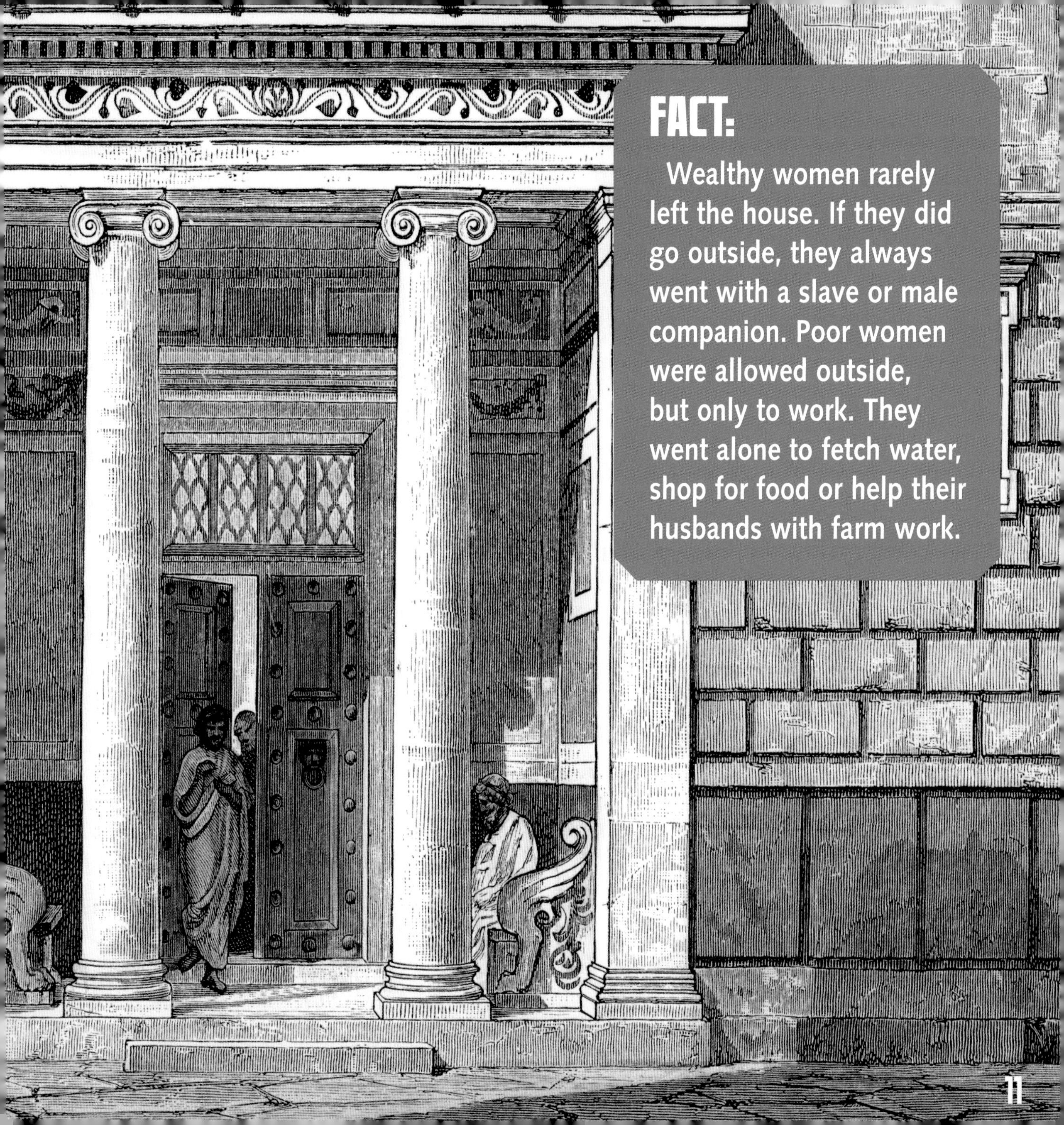

FACT:

Wealthy women rarely left the house. If they did go outside, they always went with a slave or male companion. Poor women were allowed outside, but only to work. They went alone to fetch water, shop for food or help their husbands with farm work.

Food

The ancient Greeks ate three meals a day. Fish and seafood were popular. People also ate a lot of bread, fruit, garlic and onions. Much of the food was cooked in olive oil. People ate their food with their fingers. They usually drank water or wine mixed with water.

THE IMPORTANT OLIVE TREE

Olive trees were very important to the ancient Greeks. Greeks often ate olives. They used olive oil for cooking, lighting lamps and making skin care products. Olive oil was also sold to other countries. Olympic winners' crowns were even made of olive tree leaves woven together.

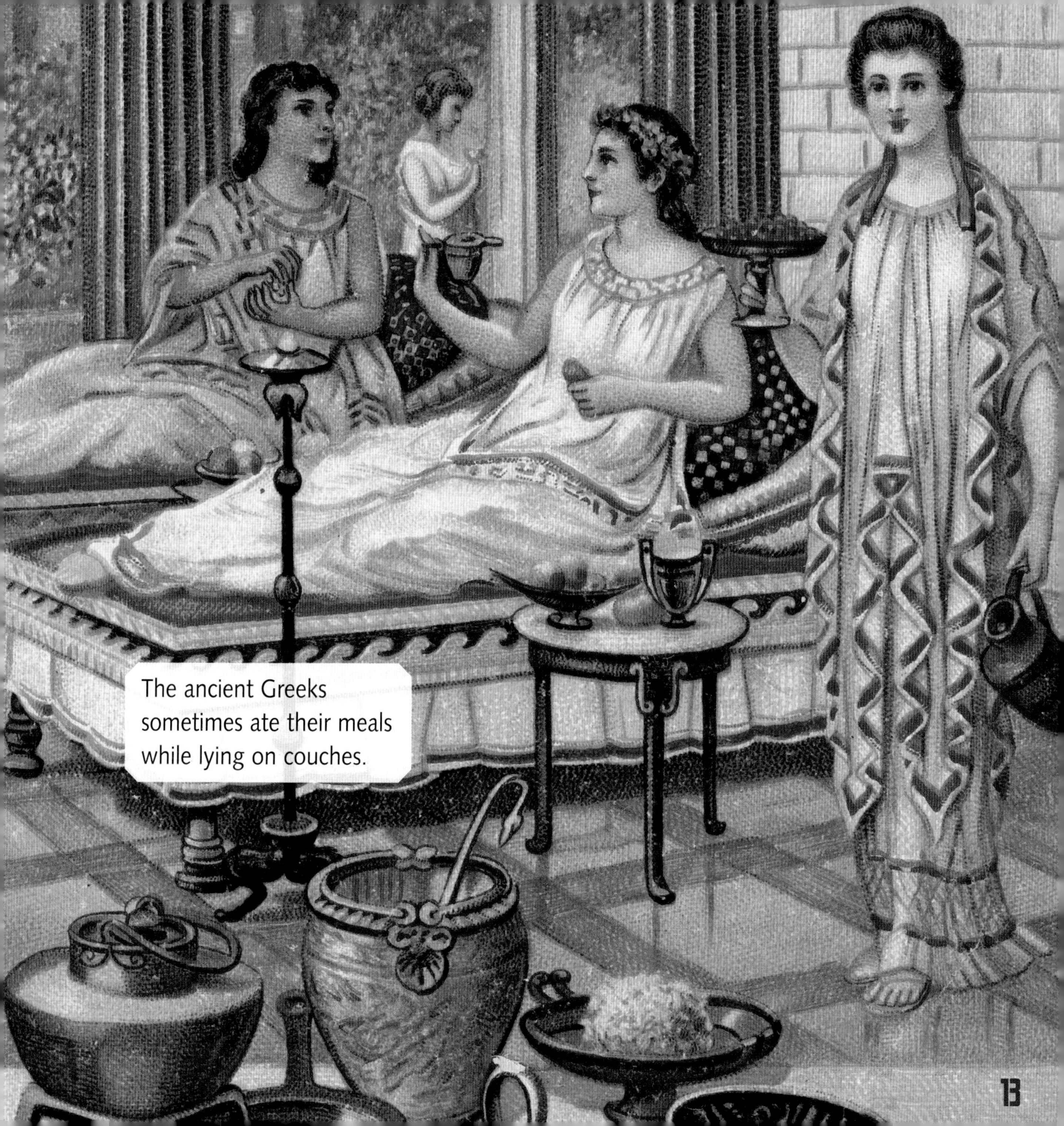

The ancient Greeks sometimes ate their meals while lying on couches.

EDUCATION AND WORK

Work

Greek men were expected to work outside the home. Many served in the military. Others worked as fishermen, farmers, **craftsmen** or artists. Farmers grew crops, such as barley and wheat, in fields close to home. Craftsmen worked in shops around the **agora**.

This vase painting shows how Greeks gathered olives.

craftsmen people who are skilled at making things with their hands

agora open marketplace in ancient Greece

Military education in Sparta

Most young Greek men went to military school at the age of 18. They trained to be soldiers or sailors in the navy. They prepared for the battles that often happened between Greek **city states**.

Military training was especially tough in the city state of Sparta. Boys were sent to live at military schools at age the age of seven. They trained very hard and had little food or clothing, no shoes and hard beds. Young men took a fitness test between the ages of 18 and 20. If a man didn't pass, he was no longer considered a citizen of Sparta.

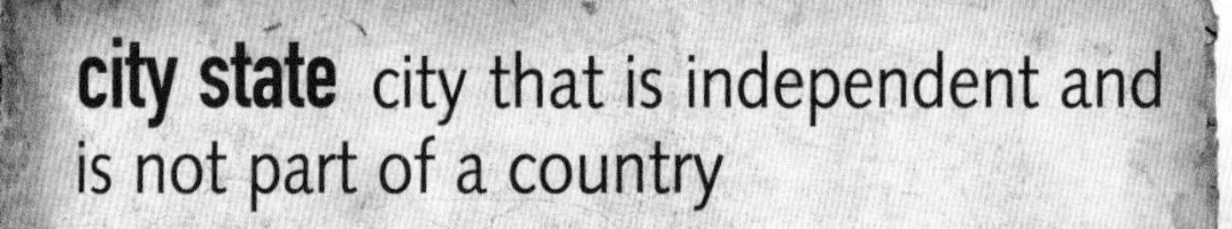
city state city that is independent and is not part of a country

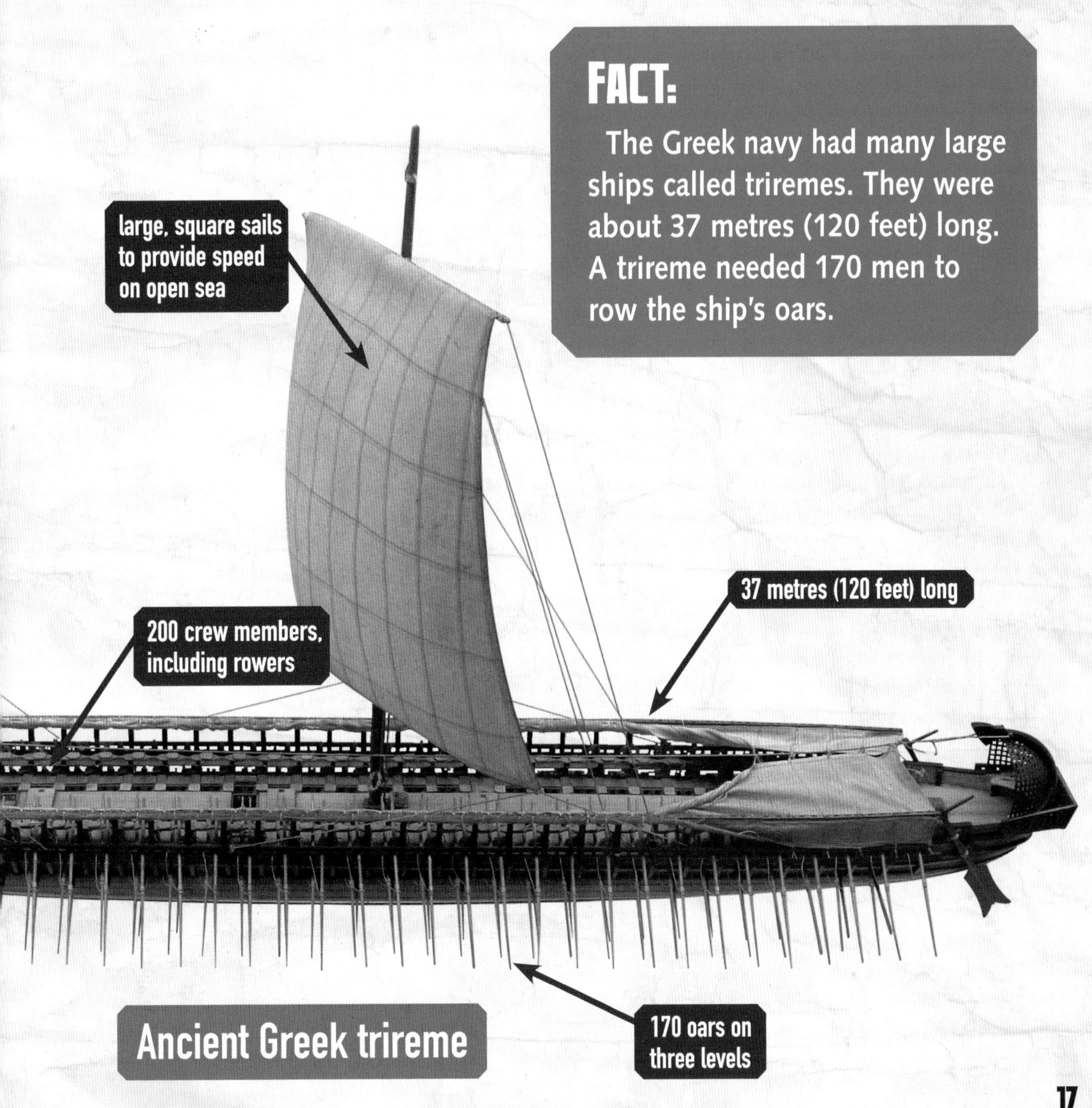

FACT:

The Greek navy had many large ships called triremes. They were about 37 metres (120 feet) long. A trireme needed 170 men to row the ship's oars.

Ancient Greek trireme

RELIGION AND THE ARTS

Honouring the gods

Religion was a big part of ancient Greek life. The Greeks believed in many gods. Many large temples were built for the gods. Each temple honoured a certain god and included a statue of the god inside. The Greeks often performed animal sacrifices and held other **ceremonies** to please their gods.

ceremony special actions, words or music performed to mark an important event

temple to the Greek god, Hephaestus

FACT:

About 80 per cent of Greek temples faced east. The Greeks wanted the rising sun to shine inside the temples during festivals.

Arts and entertainment

The ancient Greeks enjoyed several forms of entertainment. They danced, sang and played instruments, such as **lyres**. The Greeks built large, open-air theatres into hillsides. They performed plays in the theatres to honour the gods. Singers and poets also told tales of Greek heroes and gods for audiences at the theatres.

lyre small, stringed, harplike instrument

a theatre in ancient Athens

Glossary

agora open marketplace in ancient Greece

ceremony special actions, words or music performed to mark an important event

chamber pot type of bowl that people used as a toilet

city state city that is independent and is not part of a country

courtyard open area surrounded by walls

craftsmen people who are skilled at making things with their hands

lyre small, stringed, harplike instrument

sacrifice offering made to a god

slave person who is owned by another person and is forced to work without pay

stylus ancient tool with a sharp pointed end used for writing

tunic loose, sleeveless garment

tutor teacher who gives lessons to only one student or a small group of students

wealthy having a great deal of money

Read more

Ancient Greeks (Beginners), Stephanie Turnball (Usborne Publishing Ltd, 2015)

Geography Matters in Ancient Greece (Geography Matters in Ancient Civilizations) Melanie Waldron (Heinemann Raintree, 2015)

You Wouldn't Want to be a Slave in Ancient Greece!: A Life You'd Rather Not Have (You Wouldn't Want To), Fiona Macdonald (Franklin Watts, 2014)

Websites

www.ancientgreece.co.uk
Learn all about ancient Greece on The British Museum website.

www.bbc.co.uk/history/anicent/greeks/
Explore topics about ancient Greeks, such as the Olympic Games, theatres and gods.

Comprehension questions

1. The ancient Greeks believed in many gods. Name three ways in which they honoured and worshiped the gods.

2. Why do you think boys in Sparta went to live at tough military schools at such a young age?

Index